Business for Kids

A guide for kids and teens to starting a profitable business, in the words of an 11-year-old entrepreneur.

By: Finley Clough

For my Mom and Dad,
You guys are awesome!

Contents

Money, Money, Money

Before you start a business, you must understand the world of money.

One Dollar

Why is one dollar worth a dollar? Because everybody says it is! What if you started a petition that says a dollar bill is worth one hundred dollars! Now that would be interesting.

Transactions

A transaction is the passing of money from one hand to the other. Millions of transactions are made every day! When you get an allowance or when you pay for the snacks at the pool. Those are both transactions.

Loans

Loans are an important part of starting a business if you don't have your own money. A loan is where someone with extra money will loan their money to someone who needs it. The loan is eventually paid back, sometimes with interest. But be careful when you take a loan because, if your business fails you still have to pay them back. There are lots of people that will loan you money, including your parents and the bank.

Interest

Interest is the extra money you have to pay to the people that loaned you money. Usually, it is five to ten percent, but it can be more. If you don't pay it back right away, it could end up being twice the amount you were loaned! But some people don't charge interest, like your parents.

Sum it up

The world of money is like a roller coaster. Your money could go up or down, so be careful no matter what.

Business Ideas

What is a business? A business is selling a good or service for profit. Anyone can have a business, no matter how young.

How to start

Starting a business can be tricky but with the right idea, you can pull through. First, you have to think of a need. What does everybody need? Food, clothes? If you still can't think of anything, think of what everybody wants. Books, toys, candy, jewelry, sweets?

Perfect! Now you can capitalize on that idea. How could you make it special? Or how could you make it better? Now write it down, you will need this later.

Ideas

Here are some business ideas I thought of to kick start your business.

If you love horses, you could:

-Re-model model horses

-Make custom model horse tack

-Teach a younger rider who has a horse how to ride

-Muck out stalls

-Photograph horses

-Write a horse guide

If you love pets, you could:

-Pet sit

-Make pet treats

-Design pet bowls

-Become a dog walker

-Or a dog groomer

If you love crafts, you could:

-Make custom cards

-Make your own jewelry

-Sew bags

-Design scrapbooks for people who don't have the
time

-Draw pictures and sell them

If you like kids, you could

-Be a babysitter

-Start a story hour

-Teach a musical instrument

-Be a mom's helper

-Help at kid's birthday parties

If you like doing odd jobs, you could:

-Mow lawns

-Wash cars

-Become a tutor

-Have a bake sale

If you're good at something that you could make a business out of, then there is a great idea! Think about how other people could benefit from what you're selling. A critical part of a successful business is having customers that want to buy it! See if any of your family members would want to buy it and work from there.

100+ Business Ideas

1. Start a lemonade stand

2. Sell cookies

3. Enter poem contests

4. Enter writing contests

5. Enter photography contests

6. Have a bake sale

7. Make headbands

8. Make scarves

9. Design jewelry

10. Draw pictures

11. Paint pictures

12. Write a book

13. Sell coffee

14. Sell tea

15. Sell custom cars

16. Sell custom wrapping paper

17. Make chocolate

18. Make marshmallows

19. Make picture frames

20. Sell bath bombs

21. Make craft kits

22. Host a yard sale

23. Make baby mobiles

24. Make candy

25. Sell dog treats

26. Make cat bowls

27. Sell bunny toys

28. Make slime

29. Sell pictures

30. Design puzzles

31. Re-paint model toys

32. Sew cute shirts

33. Grow your own flowers

34. Illustrate a book

35. Make cool erasers

36. Knit hats

37. Arm knit scarves

38. Crochet wash clothes

39. Weave potholders

40. Create cool perler bead pictures

41. Make mosaics

42. Make your own stickers

43. Mix hand lotion

44. Sell soap

45. Design calendars

46. Grow your own veggies

47. Sew cozy blankets

48. Make trail mix

49. Sell baking mixes

50. Baby sit

51. Paint fences

52. Start a story time

53. Design someone's scrapbook

54. Be a gardener's helper

55. Be a mulcher

56. Weed flower beds

57. Paint girl's nails

58. Be a house sitter

59. Become a pet sitter

60. Walk dogs

61. Mow lawns

62. Teach piano

63. Teach a sport

64. Host art class

65. Host a writing class

66. Have a cooking class

67. Sort coupons for friends

68. Fix computers

69. Take out the garbage

70. Do laundry

71. Organize closets

72. Do a photo shoot

73. Wash cars

74. Pick up sticks

75. Rake leaves

76. Chop firewood

77. Move furniture

78. Be an elderly person's companion

79. Bring in the mail every day

80. Design and build computer programs

81. Design an app

82. Grocery shop for the elderly

83. Paint curb numbers

84. Fix bikes

85. Build dog houses

86. Trim bushes

87. Work at a local barn

88. Become a camp counselor

89. Teach swim lessons

90. Shovel snow

91. Serve food at a birthday party

92. Organize birthday parties

93. Become a referee

94. Braid hair

95. Do make up

96. Pick out someone's outfits

97. Wash windows

98. Make a coloring book

99. Make phone cases

100. Sew cute backpacks

101. Making Pet Treats

102. Making Friendship Bracelets

103. Making Decorations for a Party

104. Making Key Chains

105. Cleaning Up After Parties

106. Watering Plants

107. Packing Boxes for Moving

108. Cleaning Pools

Business Plans

Sounds boring, huh? But business plans are one of the most important parts of a business! I also think they are a lot of fun. A business plan is almost all the information that's in your head, on a piece of paper. A business plan explains a few of these things:

-What is your business called?

-What will your expenses be?

-How will you pay for these expenses?

See? These are very simple questions but, are very important. In this book, I will teach you how to answer these questions.

Why is a business plan so important? Because you will show it to your potential investors, like your parents. That way they know what you are doing with their money. Are you getting the idea?

Buying and Supplying

Most businesses take money to get started. And since you're starting a business you will need some too. So, what are your options?

Borrowing

This is a good method of getting money for starters. Borrowing is where someone gives you money and then you pay them back. It's as simple as that! NO interest and NO fees. You pay back the exact amount you borrowed.

Investors

Investors are people that give a certain amount of money for a percentage of your profit. Most investors want five to fifteen percent profit. You usually don't have to pay back your investors because they are getting money from profit. Investors are willing to pay more money if they love your business plan.

Where to find them

People to borrow from and people who want to invest aren't very hard to find. It can be anyone you know. Your parents, your uncle, your best friend, your grandparent, and your neighbor. Anybody that believes your idea is a good one.

Starting without them

If you can't or don't want to get help with finances, then here is a way to provide it yourself.

Allowance

You may or may not get an allowance, but you will need to convince your parents to give you some. Here are some ways:

-Ask your parents that if you wash dishes or mow the lawn for a week, they could give you ten dollars.

-Babysit your younger siblings for your parents

-Make them lunch or dinner

Really the only way to do it is to make your parents happy. And don't worry if they only give you one or two dollars because it adds up quickly. Another key to getting money to start up is to save your money. Try to resist going to the mall or the movies. Just think of how after your business has started making a profit, then you could go on a shopping spree!

Buying and Supplying

Think about what you'll need to start your business.

A lawn mower? Some scrapbooking supplies? Unless

you have everything, you need, you will have to go

shopping. You can look online and see the pricing.

Compare the price of the soap at one shop to the

price at the other. Before you go and pick the

cheapest one, you need to ask these questions:

Is the more expensive one better?

Does the cheap one break easily?

Is the more expensive one from a company you know

and trust?

These are important questions.

Ordering

Once you have picked out what you like the best,

you can purchase it from a local store or order it

online. Once you get your supplies you can move on

to the next step.

Starting a business without

money

If you can't find any investors or any source of money, then this is the chapter for you.

Different ideas

Since you need money to start most businesses you must think of another idea. Just look around your house for something that you're not using, such as markers, flour, and old CDs. Try to think of an idea that uses one of those items. Anything that makes money.

Once you start making money, you can invest some

more into it or start your other business.

Making money with minimal work

The best way to make money without doing any work is to sell old clothes and toys online. Just use Storenvy or eBay. Find any clothes that don't fit or that you don't like. Then take pictures. Also, you can sell your old CDs and toys that you don't want. This is the most efficient way of making money without doing any work. But you could also pay someone to do the work for you. Ask a sibling or a friend to mow your neighbor's lawn each week for five bucks.

Hopefully what they don't know is that your neighbor pays you ten dollars to mow the lawn so you are making profit. Now these are the two best ways ever! Good luck!

Budgeting

Even though your business is making a profit, you still need a budget. Instead of spending all of your money, you should put some aside for you next business.

Creating a budget

Write down how much income you make each month. (That is how much money people give you after you give them the change) Now write down how much money it cost to start your business. Don't forget to write down your investor's percentage as well. Subtract the expenses from the income and write that number down too.

If it's a positive number, good job! If it's a negative number, then you need to adjust your budget. Here's how:

Too expensive

What's too expensive? Is it the gas for the mower? Try to find another place to get your gas. Or see if there is a way to use less. Also, see if you can switch to a different material.

No income

Are you not receiving enough income? Try some more advertising tactics from the advertising chapter. Are you selling at the wrong place? Look over the Sell It chapter again. Is your product too expensive? Look at the pricing chapter once more.

If you still have a negative number, then ask your customers. They will tell you what's wrong. Once you have a positive number you need to keep it that way. You need to track your income, expenses, and profit on a piece of paper. Always write down how much you spend and make. Don't forget to write down how much profit was made each month. Now you have a good budget!

Investing

We talked a bit about investors and interest in the previous chapters. In this chapter, we will talk about how you can invest!

Stock

When you invest your money into stock, you are basically buying part of the company. One teeny tiny part. Like this much:

IIIIIIIIIIIIIIIIIIIIIIIIIIIIIIIIIIIIIIIIIIIIIIIIIIIIIIIIIIIIIIIIIIIIIIIIIIIIIIIIIIIIIIIIIIIIII

IIIIIIIIIIIIII

But the more you buy, the more you get. Exactly like this:

llllllllllllllllllllllllllllllllllllllllllllllllllllllllllllllllllllllllllllllllllllllllllll
llllllllllllllll

Let's say that you are going to invest one hundred dollars. The stock you want to invest in cost one dollar per share. You would be able to buy one hundred shares. As soon as you buy the stock, it goes up five percent. That means it goes up five cents per share. Five cents' times one hundred equals five hundred cents, or five dollars. You can wait or sell now. Let's say you wait. It goes up another fifteen percent! Each of your shares goes up twenty cents. So, you now have one hundred- and twenty-dollars' worth of shares! You better sell quick.

Congratulations, you now have one hundred and twenty dollars. Now let's pretend you bought one thousand shares. You would have made two hundred dollars in profit! Make sure you choose investments wisely because they can go down and you can lose money. Now that's how you invest.

Saving

Saving is important no matter what. You may have started a business because you are saving up for something, or you just wanted some cash. You may also want to save up to reinvest in your business. Saving is as easy as taking out an envelope, writing savings on it and putting in a dollar a week. Or even five dollars! It's as simple as that. You start with a goal and an amount that you will save every week. If you stick to your goal, you will achieve it. Here is an example:

I want a tablet that costs two hundred and fifty dollars. I can save twenty-five dollars a week. I will get my tablet in ten weeks.

Goal = $250

Amount saved per week = $25

Time until goal achieved = 10 weeks

Another way to save is to open a savings account. You can put the money in the account, and it earns interest. Now you are saving even more!

Spending

Spending is also important. If you spend all of your money, you won't be able to buy supplies for your business.

Don't spend

When you are at the mall, try not to buy everything you see. Ask yourself if you need it. If the answer is no, then don't buy it. If the answer is yes, then check around at other stores to see if it's cheaper there. If it's the cheapest one, then you can get it. Another tip to not spending is to not carry money around. If you don't have it, you can't spend it.

Only take money if you know what you're looking

for or if you have some extra spending money. And

that is how you save. I hope it helps you spend less!

Creating a Product

Now that you have your supplies pick a date to start creating or building your product. If you are selling a service, you can skip this section.

The product

What are you selling? You need to start creating it. If you are making jewelry, make some necklaces. If you're remodeling model horses, re-model some. After you've made some you can test them out. Wear one of your headbands for a day. Did it snap? Well, if it did you need to figure out how to fix it.

You want your customers to be happy, so make it the best you can. If you have different varieties of your product, make some of those too. Like if you have a pet treat business, don't just make dog treats, make cat treats as well.

Picture Perfect

After you have all your different products ready, you need to take pictures. Pictures are perfect for, flyers, business cards, and websites. So, make sure you have the best ones.

Don't worry about making a bunch of each product. One or two of each will do fine. But we'll talk about that in the next chapter.

Time and Stock

Time is also an important part of a business. If you

don't have time to make your product or do your

service, you can't have a business. How much time

do you have? Two hours a day? Three days a week?

This is another thing to add in your business plan.

Stock

Stock is what we talked a little bit about in the last chapter. When a business is starting off, it doesn't know what will sell the best. So you only need a few products. But even though you only need a few completed doesn't mean you shouldn't order more supplies! If you ever run out of products, don't forget to make more.

Selling a Service

If you happened to think of a service for your business, then this is the chapter for you!

Selling

Let's say that Mrs. Johnson wants her lawn mowed on Wednesday at two o'clock. First, make sure you have the time. No piano lessons or trips to grandma's house. Next, make sure you have the transportation. Maybe you can ride your bike, or in your parent's car. After that, you need to make sure you have the supplies. In this case, you will need a lawn mower.

If all the previous steps are clear, you can move on to the next step.

Service

So now you're arriving at Mrs. Johnson's house on the desired date at the desired time. Go ahead and knock on the door. Tell her you are ready to mow the lawn. If she is absent go ahead and start working. Once you start the service, you need to the best job you can. After the job or service is completed tell Mrs. Johnson how much it cost. If she is still absent, leave a note or invoice and you are done! Don't forget to thank your client the next time you see them.

Happy Customers

Keeping your customers happy is key if you want more sales. If they're happy they will tell their friends.

Broken

If one of your customers says that one on the charms that you sold her had snapped in half, you should just apologize, make her a new one, and give her a special coupon. Problem solved!

Correction

If one of the moms that you help tells you that you're making the sandwiches wrong, don't get upset. Do what you are told and do it the best you can. And don't complain! Save your complaining for your own mom.

Happy

The number one thing to do to keep you customers happy is to smile. Smiling will make you happy and that will make your customer happy too.

Sell it

This chapter talks about some of the best places to sell your products and services.

Craft shows

Craft shows are one of the best places to sell your products, but not so much your services. Most craft shows will only take people that sell homemade products. Most craft shows are around 25 to 50 dollars for a table. Just be sure you will make about two times what you spend for the table.

Once you find a craft show you should sign up and prepare. You never know how much you will sell so make as many as you can.

On the day of the craft show, you should go early to set up ad set out your products. Whenever you see a potential customer you should smile and shake their hand. Even if they walk by without buying anything, don't get discouraged. There will probably be one hundred people walking by your stand. And don't forget, have fun doing it!

Yard sales

Yard sales are a great way for selling cookies or lemonade. If people don't see anything they want, they might get a treat.

Farmers markets

Farmers markets are a lot different from craft shows, farmers markets sell a lot of produce and baked goods. When you buy a stand at a farmer's market you go every week instead of once. A farmer's market is probably a little more expensive than a craft show.

Parks

If you sell at a park in the summer, you will probably get a lot of customers. Selling lemonade to all the hot and sweaty people will make a lot of money. Or you could sell dog treats at a dog park. Now those are good ideas.

Neighborhoods

Selling in your neighborhood is a great way to sell services. The customers are just a couple houses away. You can make flyers or make business cards to hand out. There are many ways to sell in your neighborhood.

Sell it online

There are many ways to sell your products online. If you are selling a service, you should skip this chapter. If you've made it this far and finally found out your business won't work. There is an alternate solution.

Blogging

Many website builders have the option to add a blog to your website. You could add a blog to your website and post about your product, or just have a blog and put ads on it.

Cost

The cost of starting a business can be cheap if you're willing to have a surname. It can be about five to ten dollars a month or free forever. It's your call. Even though your website might be free, you may have to pay to add a web store to it.

Etsy

If you don't want to design your own website, selling on Etsy is a great idea. Etsy basically lets you make your own product page on their website. It cost twenty cents for each product you're selling. So, if you're selling five cat treats, that's 1 dollar. Your product is up for four months then if it doesn't sell, then it's taken down. So, make sure your product sells. Other than that, it's a great website to sell on.

Storenvy

This is a website just like Etsy. But it isn't as geared towards crafts. It's also a little cheaper. Storenvy gets ten percent of your profit. So, if you don't sell, you don't pay.

eBay

eBay is a good website to sell your old clothes and toys. This is the most expensive of the three, but a lot of people shop on it.

Creating a website

When creating a website, you can choose from lots of different themes and colors. As you go along you can edit the theme you picked or pick a new one. You can add your own text, your own pictures, and a blog if you want. There is so much you can do. Keep on dreaming!

Advertise

Advertising is a great way to get you and your business out there.

YouTube

If you have a YouTube channel, a great way to start advertising would be telling your YouTube fans about your business. Give them links to your website in the description and encourage them to start their own business. If you put ads on your videos you could get a lot of money. Also, if you have a lot of subscribers. You can watch other videos to get more ideas. Or even start a video blog.

Buying ads

This can get very expensive but it's very effective.

When designing your ads, don't leave out any details

even the bad ones. Tell them the features, ingredients

and why yours is the best. It's also fun to choose

colors for your ads and pick what websites it's on.

You can also get ads in magazines, newspapers, and

newsletters. The cost varies by where you're putting

your ad, how big it is and when you're putting it out.

If you put an ad up around Christmas time, it might

be more expensive than in the spring.

Flyers and cards

Flyers and business cards are great to hand out or hang in store windows. When you are designing business cards there are some no goes.

-Don't put your address on

-Don't put your picture on

But most things are a must:

-Put your name on

-Put your business' name on

-Put your logo on

-Put your service or product on

-Put on your contact information

Once you have all of that on your business card, you can print them out.

The Word of Mouth

The word of mouth is the cheapest. Just kindly ask your clients to tell their friends and so on.

Traffic

After you have completed at least one of these ways to advertise, you should be getting more traffic. So keep advertising!

Pricing

Pricing is important because you don't want to lose money by not charging enough and you don't want to scare away customers by charging too much.

Cost

How much did the materials cost? Let's say that you knit hats. It cost five dollars for one ball of yarn. And you can make two hats out of one ball. The cost of making one hat, is two dollars and fifty cents. If it takes you one hour to knit a hat. That's about one dollar and a half of time. Two dollars and fifty cents plus one dollar and fifty cents equal four dollars.

In order to make a profit you need to make more money than you spend by at least half. So the price of your product is six dollars! And that's how you price your product. To price your service just cut out the part about expenses unless you have any.

Finish

Now it's time to send your product or service into the world of money! Good luck!

What not to do

Not getting any sales? You are probably doing

something on this list:

Do not:

Go with the cheapest materials

Sit back and relax at a craft show

Mess around and not complete your job

Partially make your product

Advertise only once

Spend all the money that's for your business

Stop making products

If you realize you are doing any of these things, you should quickly solve the problems. If you aren't, then good job!

Expanding

Has your business made a lot of money? Do you want to make more? This chapter talks about expanding.

More products

A good way of getting more customers is making different kinds of products. Continue thinking of different ideas of different products and make one or two.

More places

If you currently sell at craft shows, you could think about selling at a farmers' markets too. Or you could sell online also.

More customers

To get more customers, you need to reach different kinds of people. If you currently sell to kids, then think about also selling to adults or vice-versa. Try to think of where you could market to those people.

My Businesses

Now since I'm writing this book about businesses, I should tell you about mine.

F.C.C

Finley's custom cards was my favorite business. I would pass out flyers to my neighbors and they would fill out the form on the back. I would then create a card based on what they wanted. I didn't get a lot of customers because we live in a small neighborhood, but I did make a profit.

Home sweet tea

The idea never became a business. The idea was that when someone ordered tea off my website, I would buy the tea and the flavorings and put them in jars. Then I would send it to the person. The reason this never became a business, was because I didn't have enough time.

Kate the Detective

This was my very first business. I had recently received a typewriter for my birthday, so I started typing out stories and copying them. I then sold them to neighbors. I made five dollars, which was a lot to me. I stopped selling them because I couldn't keep selling the same thing to the same people. I still have a couple of stories from that. I thought it was a fun business.

Finley's Rainbow looms

This is my most recent business idea. I started this business about three months ago, and it's really progressed. This website sells rainbow loom bracelets and I'm thinking about adding some charms too. This business has made some profit so far. I can't wait to see where it goes! Feel free to use any of these ideas!

Everything?

Even though money is in a lot of different places, that doesn't mean it's everything. Money is of some importance like you need to buy food and provide air conditioning. It can also be spent on fun things like that new video game or a shopping spree. But there are countries where people live on a dollar a day. There are many ways to help people like that. You can donate to foundations that support these people. To them, money isn't everything. Everything to them is staying alive. Life is hard and money makes it harder. So many decisions! Should I buy that piece of candy? Should I not? Also, don't count on money to bail to help you out of sticky situations.

Money is always going to run out. You must keep working for it, and don't spend it every chance you get. So good luck!

Thank you!

Thank you so much for reading this book. I hope it helps you with your business. If you are stuck and need more ideas, please read my next book about how to write a book. It's coming out in the winter of 2017. So, check that out. I used many of these ideas to start my business. Please tell your friends about this book. Thank you! -Finley

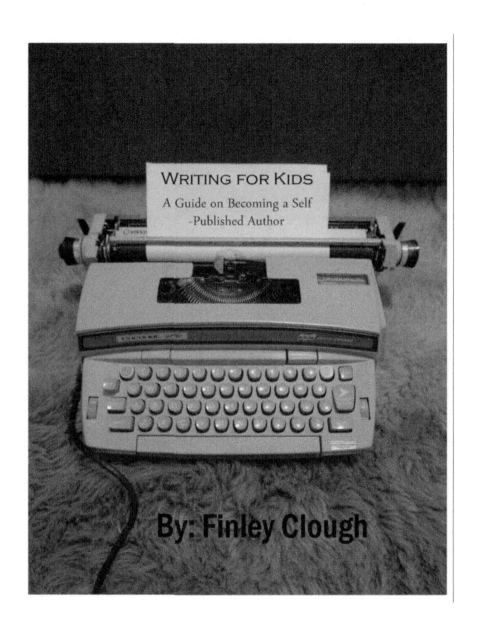

Keep an eye out for my new
book: Writing for Kids!